COMMANDS OF KALI LINUX

COMMANDS

PAVAN KUMAR NALLURI

XpressPublishing
An imprint of Notion Press

Old No. 38, New No. 6
McNichols Road, Chetpet
Chennai - 600 031

First Published by Notion Press 2020
Copyright © Pavan Kumar Nalluri 2020
All Rights Reserved.

ISBN 978-1-64892-904-5

Contents

1
Commands of KALI LINUX

WRITTEN BY
PAVANKUMAR NALLURI

<u>Common use A-Z of Kali Linux commands are here below :</u>

(A)
apropos :   Search Help manual pages (man -k)

apt:-get Search for and install software packages (Debian)

aptitude: Search for and install software packages (Debian)

aspell: Spell Checker

awk :Find and Replace text, database sort/validate/index

(B)

basename : Strip directory and suffix from filenames

bash : GNU Bourne-Again SHell

bc :Arbitrary precision calculator language

bg :Send to background

break: Exit from a loop

builtin: Run a shell builtin

bzip2: Compress or decompress named file(s)

(C)
 cal :Display a calendar

case :Conditionally perform a command

cat : Concatenate and print (display) the content of files

cd : Change Directory

cfdisk : Partition table manipulator for Linux

chgrp : Change group ownership

chmod : Change access permissions

chown : Change file owner and group

chroot : Run a command with a different root directory

chkconfig : System services (runlevel)

cksum: Print CRC checksum and byte counts

clear : Clear terminal screen

cmp : Compare two files

comm : Compare two sorted files line by line

command: Run a command - ignoring shell functions

continue : Resume the next iteration of a loop

cp :Copy one or more files to another location

cron: Daemon to execute scheduled commands

crontab: Schedule a command to run at a later time

csplit :Split a file into context-determined pieces

cut :Divide a file into several parts

(D)
date :Display or change the date time

dc :Desk Calculator

?

dd : Convert and copy a file, write disk headers, boot records

ddrescue : Data recovery tool

declare : Declare variables and give them attributes

df : Display free disk space

diff: Display the differences between two files

diff3: Show differences among three files

dig :DNS lookup

dir :Briefly list directory contents

dircolors: Colour setup for `ls`

dirname : Convert a full pathname to just a path

dirs : Display list of remembered directories

dmesg : Print kernel driver messages

du : Estimate file space usage

(E)

echo : Display message on screen

egrep : Search file(s) for lines that match an extended expression

eject : Eject removable media

enable : Enable and disable builtin shell commands

env : Environment variables

ethtool : Ethernet card settings

eval : Evaluate several commands/arguments

exec : Execute a command
?

exit : Exit the shell

expect : Automate arbitrary applications accessed over a terminal expand : Convert tabs to spaces

export : Set an environment variable

expr : Evaluate expressions

(F)

false : Do nothing, unsuccessfully

fdformat : Low-level format a floppy disk

fdisk : Partition table manipulator for Linux

fg : Send job to foreground

fgrep : Search file(s) for lines that match a fixed string

file : Determine file type

find : Search for files that meet a desired criteria

fmt : Reformat paragraph text

fold : Wrap text to fit a specified width.

for : Expand words, and execute commands

format: Format disks or tapes

free ;Display memory usage

fsck: File system consistency check and repair

ftp : File Transfer Protocol

function : Define Function Macros

?

fuser : Identify/kill the process that is accessing a file

(G)

gawk : Find and Replace text within file(s)

getopts : Parse positional parameters

grep : Search file(s) for lines that match a given pattern

groupadd : Add a user security group

groupdel : Delete a group

groupmod: Modify a group

groups : Print group names a user is in

gzip : Compress or decompress named file(s)

(H)
hash : Remember the full pathname of a name argument

head : Output the first part of file(s)

help : Display help for a built-in command

history : Command History

hostname : Print or set system name

(I)

iconv : Convert the character set of a file

id : Print user and group id's

if :Conditionally perform a command

ifconfig : Configure a network interface

ifdown : Stop a network interface

?

ifup : Start a network interface up

import : Capture an X server screen and save the image to file

install : Copy files and set attributes

(J)

jobs : List active jobs

join : Join lines on a common field

(K)

kill : Stop a process from running

killall: Kill processes by name

(L)

less : Display output one screen at a time

let : Perform arithmetic on shell variables

ln : Create a symbolic link to a file

local : Create variables

locate : Find files

logname : Print current login name

logout : Exit a login shell

look : Display lines beginning with a given string

lpc: Line printer control program

lpr : Off line print

lprint : Print a file

lprintd : Abort a print job
?

lprintq : List the print queue

lprm : Remove jobs from the print queue

ls :List information about file(s)

lsof : List open files

(M)

make : Recompile a group of programs

man : Help manual

mkdir : Create new folder(s)

mkfifo : Make FIFOs (named pipes)

mkisofs : Create an hybrid ISO9660/JOLIET/HFS filesystem

mknod : Make block or character special files

more : Display output one screen at a time

mount : Mount a file system

mtools : Manipulate MS-DOS files

mtr : Network diagnostics (traceroute/ping)

mv : Move or rename files or directories

mmv : Mass Move and rename (files)

(N)

netstat : Networking information

nice : Set the priority of a command or job

nl : Number lines and write files

?

nohup : Run a command immune to hangups

notify:-send Send desktop notifications

nslookup : Query Internet name servers interactively

(O)

open : Open a file in its default application

op :Operator access

(P)

passwd : Modify a user password

paste :Merge lines of files

pathchk : Check file name portability

ping :Test a network connection

pkill : Stop processes from running

popd : Restore the previous value of the current directory

pr : Prepare files for printing

printcap : Printer capability database

printenv: Print environment variables

printf : Format and print data

ps : Process status

pushd: Save and then change the current directory

pwd :Print Working Directory

(Q)

quota : Display disk usage and limits
??

quotacheck : Scan a file system for disk usage

quotactl : Set disk quotas

(R)

ram : ram disk device

rcp :Copy files between two machines

read :Read a line from standard input

readarray : Read from stdin into an array variable

readonly : Mark variables/functions as readonly

reboot : Reboot the system

rename : Rename files

renice : Alter priority of running processes

remsync : Synchronize remote files via email

return : Exit a shell function

rev : Reverse lines of a file
rm : Remove files

rmdir : Remove folder(s)

rsync: Remote file copy (Synchronize file trees)

(S)

screen :Multiplex terminal, run remote shells via ssh

scp : Secure copy (remote file copy)

sdiff : Merge two files interactively

sed : Stream Editor
??

select : Accept keyboard input

seq : Print numeric sequences

set : Manipulate shell variables and functions

sftp : Secure File Transfer Program

shift : Shift positional parameters

shopt : Shell Options

shutdown : Shutdown or restart linux

sleep : Delay for a specified time

slocate: Find files

sort : Sort text files

source : Run commands from a file `.'

split : Split a file into fixed-size pieces

ssh : Secure Shell client (remote login program)

strace : Trace system calls and signals

su ; Substitute user identity

sudo : Execute a command as another user

sum : Print a checksum for a file

suspend : Suspend execution of this shell

symlink : Make a new name for a file

sync : Synchronize data on disk with memory

 (T)
??

tail : Output the last part of file

tar : Tape ARchiver

tee : Redirect output to multiple files

test : Evaluate a conditional expression

time : Measure Program running time

times :User and system times

touch : Change file timestamps

top : List processes running on the system

traceroute : Trace Route to Host

trap : Run a command when a signal is set(bourne)

tr : Translate, squeeze, and/or delete characters

true : Do nothing, successfully

tsort : Topological sort

tty : Print filename of terminal on stdin

type : Describe a command

(U)

ulimit : Limit user resources

umask : Users file creation mask

umount : Unmount a device

unalias : Remove an alias

uname : Print system information

??

unexpand : Convert spaces to tabs

uniq : Uniquify files

units : Convert units from one scale to another

unset : Remove variable or function names

unshar : Unpack shell archive scripts

until : Execute commands (until error)

uptime : Show uptime

useradd : Create new user account

userdel : Delete a user account

usermod : Modify user account

users : List users currently logged in

uuencode : Encode a binary file

uudecode : Decode a file created by uuencode

(v)

v : Verbosely list directory contents (`ls -l -b`)

vdir : Verbosely list directory contents (`ls -l -b`)

vi : Text Editor

vmstat: Report virtual memory statistics

(w)

wait : Wait for a process to complete

watch: Execute/display a program periodically

wc :Print byte, word, and line counts
??

whereis : Search the user's $path, man pages and source files for a program

which : Search the user's $path for a program file

while : Execute commands

who : Print all usernames currently logged in

whoami : Print the current user id and name (`id -un`)

wget : Retrieve web pages or files via HTTP, HTTPS or FTP

write : Send a message to another user

(x)

xargs : Execute utility, passing constructed argument list(s)

xdg:-open Open a file or URL in the user's preferred application.

yes : Print a string until interrupted

Some Exanples:
Command: ls
The command "ls" stands for (List Directory Contents), List the contents of the folder, be it file or folder, from which it runs. The most common options are -a (all files) and -l (long or details) Tab completion is supported and may be configured with .inputrc

When output to file the files are listed one per line. By default, colour is not used to distinguish types of files. That is equivalent to using --color=none. Using the --color option without the optional WHEN argument is equivalent to using --color=always. With --color=auto, color codes are output only if standard output is connected to a terminal (tty).
??

Command: lsblk
The "lsblk" stands for (List Block Devices), print block devices by their assigned name (but not RAM) on the standard output in a tree-like fashion.

he "lsblk -l" command list block devices in „list„ structure (not tree like Note: lsblk is very useful and easiest way to know the name of New Usb Device you just plugged in, especially when you have to deal with disk/blocks in terminal.

Command: sudo
he "sudo" (super user do) command allows a permitted user to execute a command as the superuser or another user, as specified by the security policy in the sudoers list.
exp: root@Kali:~# sudo add-apt-repository ppa:tualatrix/ppa

Note: sudo allows user to borrow superuser privileged, while a similar command „su„ allows user to actually log in as superuser. Sudo is safer than su.
It is not advised to use sudo or su for day-to-day normal use, as it can result in serious error if accidentally you did something wrong, that"s why
a very popular saying in Linux community is:

"To err is human, but to really foul up everything, you need root password."
??

 Command: mkdir
The "mkdir" (Make directory) command create a new directory with name path. However is the directory already exists, it will return an error message "cannot create folder, folder already exists".
exp: root@Kalitut:~# mkdir Kalitut .

Note: Directory can only be created inside the folder, in which the user has write permission. mkdir: cannot create directory `Kalitut„: File exists (Don"t confuse with file in the above output, you might remember what i said at the beginning – In Linux every file, folder, drive, command, scripts are treated as file).

Command: chmod
The Linux "chmod" command stands for (change file mode bits). chmod changes the file mode (permission) of each given file, folder, script, etc.. according to mode asked for.
There exist 3 types of permission on a file (folder or anything but to keep

things simple we will be using file).

   Read (r)=4

   Write(w)=2

   Execute(x)=1

So if you want to give only read permission on a file it will be assigned a value of „4‚‚ for write permission only, a value of „2‚ and for execute

permission only, a value of „1‚ is to be given. For read and write permission 4+2 = „6‚ is to be given, ans so on.

Now permission need to be set for 3 kinds of user and usergroup. The first is owner, then usergroup and finally world.

   rwxr-x--x abc.sh

Here the root"s permission is rwx (read, write and execute).

usergroup to which it belongs, is r-x (read and execute only, no write permission) and

for world is –x (only execute).

??

To change its permission and provide read, write and execute permission to owner, group and world.

   root@Kali:~# chmod 777 abc.sh

only read and write permission to all three.

   root@Kalitut:~# chmod 666 abc.sh

read, write and execute to owner and only execute to group and world.

   root@Kalitut:~# chmod 711 abc.sh

Note: one of the most important command useful for sysadmin and user both. On a multi-user environment or on a server, this command comes to

rescue, setting wrong permission will either makes a file inaccessible or provide unauthorized access to someone.

Command: tar

The "tar" command is a Tape Archive is useful in creation of archive, in a number of file format and their extraction.

   root@Kali:~# tar -zxvf abc.tar.gz (Remember 'z' for .tar.gz)

   root@Kali:~# tar -jxvf abc.tar.bz2 (Remember 'j' for .tar.bz2)

   root@Kali:~# tar -cvf archieve.tar.gz(.bz2) /path/to/folder/abc

Note: A „tar.gz‚ means gzipped. „tar.bz2‚ is compressed with bzip which uses a better but slower compression method.

Command: cp

The "copy" stands for (Copy), it copies a file from one location to another location.

   root@Kali:~# cp /home/user/Downloads abc.tar.gz /home/user/Desktop (Return 0 when sucess)

Note: cp is one of the most commonly used command in shell scripting and it can be used with wildcard characters (Describe in the above block), for customised and desired file copying.

Command: mv

??

The "mv" command moves a file from one location to another location.

   root@Kali:~# mv /home/user/Downloads abc.tar.gz /home/user/Desktop (Return 0 when sucess)

Note: mv command can be used with wildcard characters. mv should be used with caution, as moving of system/unauthorised file may lead to security as well as breakdown of system.

Command: pwd

The command "pwd" (print working directory), prints the current working directory with full path name from terminal.

   root@Kali:~# pwd

   /home/user/Desktop

Note: This command won"t be much frequently used in scripting but it is an absolute life saver for newbie who gets lost in terminal in their early connection with nux. (Linux is most commonly referred as nux or nix).

Command: cd

Finally, the frequently used "cd" command stands for (change directory), it change the working directory to execute, copy, move write, read, etc. from terminal itself.

   root@Kali:~# cd /home/user/Desktop

   server@localhost:~$ pwd

   /home/user/Desktop

Note: cd comes to rescue when switching between directories from terminal. "Cd ~" will change the working directory to user"s home directory, and is very useful if a user finds himself lost in terminal. "Cd .." will change the working directory to parent directory (of current working directory).

Top of Form

Bottom of Form